I0542668

Praise for
Bum Knees and Grieving Sunsets

Daniel Romo is a five-tool poet. Rarely have I read poems that seamlessly integrate sports and love, religion and natural law, vulnerability and strength. *Bum Knees and Grieving Sunsets* is stacked with ear-conscious lines that have heart-conscious intentions. This is a beautiful poetry that has the largesse of a Dodger dog and had me looking at the ceiling and muttering to myself as if I was Fernando Valenzuela, which to me is the highest of praises.

— **David Tomas Martinez**, author of
Post Traumatic Hood Disorder

In *Bum Knees and Grieving Sunsets*, Daniel Romo offers incisive commentary on modern life, from the perspective of a father, spouse, teacher, sports fan, and observer of the world at its best and worst. Whether he's watching a child attempt to throw strikes, thinking about faith in the midst of an everyday scene, or pondering the power of muscle memory, Romo's speaker is a steady guide, unafraid to approach tough questions. Replete with wit, irony, and play, these poems leave the reader in a place of contemplation, as in "Proof of Life" we're told, "We do the best with what we can and call it / learning. // We hug our own bodies tight and call it / damage control."

— **Mary Biddinger**, author of
Department of Elegy

The poems in Daniel Romo's new collection wholeheartedly remind us of our "lonely stretch" of life. Every poem offers a domestic experience where "pain is never drawn to scale"— with metaphors and meditations about love and aging. A hybrid of prose and lineated poetry, these scenarios are in the voice of a father, teacher, husband, and more. In a poignant moment, Romo admits, "I'm still learning how to navigate the terrain between / fatherhood and second wife." These poems tackle life's biggest challenges with a fine balance between pathos and humor.

— **Ruben Quesada**, editor of
Latinx Poetics: Essays on the Art of Poetry

BUM KNEES &
GRIEVING SUNSETS

FLOWERSONG
P R E S S

poems by
DANIEL ROMO

This book was made possible by the generosity of "Dr. Enrique E. Figueroa's GenteChicana/SOYmosChicanos Arts Fund, which is a Donor Advised Fund at the Greater Milwaukee Foundation".

*Again I looked and saw all the oppression
that was taking place under the sun.*

— Ecclesiastes 4:1

CONTENTS

Men at forty
Learn to close softly
The doors to rooms they will not be
Coming back to.

— Donald Justice

BUM KNEES & GRIEVING SUNSETS

Front Page

The president pulled his army's troops from a
Middle Eastern country because their soldiers

were always high and didn't fight like a terrorist
takeover was imminent. So his critics find a new

way to say we're still mad our candidate lost, while
his supporters say it's okay to retreat from a war

that's not ours, and those in the middle simultaneously
snack on Nutella and curse the world. Some say these

are the end times and some's parents and entire
bloodline have said that throughout their lives

and the family that incorrectly appraises together,
stays together. What we really need is a cease fire

amongst our neighbor's head and our other neighbor's
heart, but we're too bothered by the tree hanging over

our fence that keeps dropping rotten oranges into our
backyard, though to clean up your own mess implies

the ability to both recognize and respond to untidiness.
We collect bodies that fall too early, and we gather the

overripe produce from the earth and each time the
sadness that sifts between our hands is replanted in

the forms of warnings we never heed. "Impeach him!"
"Re-elect him!" "Damnit if we're not all in trouble…"

Zenith

The veteran wrestler who headlined events for thirty years
and the glitzy, rock star pastor who admitted he had an affair

are both stepping down to focus on their families. One with
a history of hurling his opponents off the top of the steel cage,

bloodied and broken, as if directing the effects of gravity upon
bodies straddling the line between persona and perception, and

one who fought and lost with narcissism, forgetting he is also
part of the choir to which he preaches. There is no way to play

God when the outcome is already scripted, and living a double
life only works if the character and audience are both in on the

storyline. But the way to determine if it's a sport isn't by deeming
it fake or real, but by the way a man humbles himself in the loss

and how he resurrects from the rubble. A tombstone piledriver
or revelation of moral failures, even the most spirit-filled sermon

doesn't ease the blow or help prepare a man for an unexpected
fall when he loses his way down from the peak of the mountain

he's already named after himself. Because when a man loses his
way, he wanders around his own familiar landscapes attempting

to climb back up to the pinnacle of a ministry, or vocation, or steel cage, to once again have his hands raised in a sign of

victory or submission as if closer to touching Heaven.

What You Wouldn't Believe but Should

Tonight while reading my students' homework I learned
whales can get sunburned, and the average person will
spend six months of their life waiting for red lights to turn green,
and during this election season, it's difficult to distinguish
just exactly what are the facts and whose opinions mean most
to voters who don't even know the inventor of the Frisbee
was actually turned into a Frisbee after he died.
Most of the kids' grades are low yet just because I'm their
favorite teacher doesn't guarantee a free pass, although
movie trailers originally played after the movie so perhaps
I should consider giving credit before their work is even due.
I know I will not vote for the candidate who has told more than
20,000 factchecked lies in the time it takes for a school year to
begin… and end… and begin again, but I didn't know Scotland
has 421 words for snow and maybe if Arturo had confessed,
"I'm sorry, Mr. Romo. My paper got lost in a January *flindrikin*
and I just couldn't seem to find it after shoveling the driveway,"
I would be more understanding in its absence.
The CIA has its own Starbucks, but the baristas don't write
customers' names on the cups and after work I labor over
writing poems so I can appreciate anonymity in the name of
protecting one's personal and work life all in one.
But damnit if it isn't nice to be recognized for what you do,
to be saluted for giving all you got even when you're not certain
you possessed very much to begin with.
Tomorrow I will grade some more papers and even though I teach
English and not Biology, I might start a unit called *Auditory Benevolence*

in which I start by telling the kids to close their eyes and place
a hand over their chest because if they listen hard enough, they can
hear a blue whale's heartbeat from two miles away, and if he can be
that big and passionate about navigating through life,
so can we all.

Variations

You think when it rains the water's too heavy to absorb and
pours down upon your neck in an effort to snap in half what's

left of a season in which you can't tell if you're flailing in the
midst of drowning, or dying of thirst during the famine, but

either way, funeral arrangements must be made by the one
you've confided in when your hands were raised in some

form of surrender. We coddle *hurt* and nurture it as if the
plural form of the word is the lethal version when anyone

whose flesh and bones have ever ached knows less is always
more. How often we sit alone when our brokenness and

self-pity align. How frequently woe-ing is me-ing requires
the opposite of illumination to grow. It crosses your mind

why pain doesn't exist in moderation, how the core of a
man can be so easily led by an array of answers that are

all incorrect. The most difficult comprehension questions
aren't posed by a professor of a subject you've never heard

of, but by yourself, and maybe it's not a case of understanding
everything as much as it is a case of everything understanding

you. I visited a new church and learned there are bag checks
at the door and snipers on the rooftops and I'm wondering

if bullets raining down upon a man trying to harm a pastor or parishioners is mentioned in the book of Revelations.

I suppose it all comes down personal preference. Would you rather walk by a beautiful, plastic orchid sitting in the

center of your coffee table that requires closer examination for any guest to know it's not real, or would you prefer to

close your eyes and breathe in the scent of what's left of a once striking flower whose now browning petals used to be

such a divine royal purple, you'd have thought you were inhaling a whole kingdom.

Sign Stealing

I know the game has passed me by
when I'm more interested in the scandal
    than the sport.
I no longer know who's in first or last place,
but through my personal losses, I've learned how
to let go and lose with humility
and grace.
But today there is intrigue in the revelation that
the batters wore wires taped to their chests
beneath jerseys identifying the city
they repped.
There is disappointment in the way their bodies were
privy to each pitch
by some videoman in a hallway who buzzed them
    once for fastball,
    and twice for off speed,
a stolen code alerting to the curveballs
life throws.

        Because knowing the velocity of an object
        headed towards you
        doesn't teach you how to live during dry seasons of
        a swing and a miss.

I will marry my fiancée in a few months
and that is a pitch I never saw coming
because even the most sophisticated
technological advances
couldn't have alerted me
that my next at-bat after my divorce

wouldn't be the final time I was able to
spit in the ground,
dig into the box,
and stare the pitcher down as if he knew
I'd be ready.
no matter what he threw.

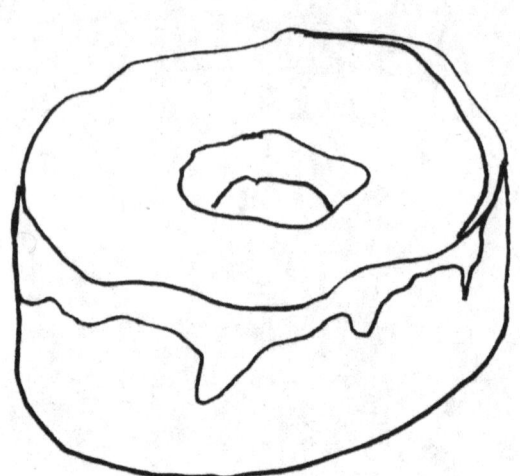

Hi Five

Robert asked how much I benched and said he was
impressed with the bulk that is my shoulders and
chest as I exited the donut shop and headed for my
car, and he mentioned how he wanted to have my
build but he's 6'3"and wiry and won state in '82
just before he enlisted. He shadowboxed the way
I could use my body to pummel another man with
hooks to the gut and face if I wanted to because
my strength is compact like his boy Sato who was
about my height and weight and whom he served
with right after high school. I wasn't familiar with
many of the MMA fighters or NBA semi-star
centers or Cuban boxers he began referring to,
but I stood partway into the street while he stood
on the sidewalk where he also slept, and I simply
listened to Robert because it was apparent no one
else ever did. I wanted to call my wife after half
an hour to tell her not to worry, I got my donut
but was helping another man relive moments
where he cheered for the accomplishments of
others and when others cheered for him. It's not
every day that you meet someone who knows
that Waymon Tisdale averaged 15 points a game
before retiring to play a mean bass and even
though he was the star of the '88 World Series,
Hershizer was on crack which Robert knew
because his sister's friend Felicia who graduated
in '91 and did hair in a not so nice part of L.A.
sold to him. And even though I hadn't ever had
that in-depth a lesson in such a variety of sports,

I just wanted to go home to eat my chocolate
donut before work like I always did. But I knew
I couldn't be like Fran Tarkenton, who Robert
says was the best scrambling quarterback ever
and could weave his way through a Buffalo
blizzard. I had to be more like Terry Bradshaw,
an immobile object who took vicious shots from
linebackers in order to deliver a perfect pass
because that's what good teammates do, and
because when I finally left, Robert shook my
hand and said we were now friends.

The Park of Pretentiousness

If you pretend not to know the homeless sleep under the trees like an evergreen canopy, you can still claim your community possesses the most pristine parks this side of Heaven. Any encampment bound by poverty isn't even worth acknowledging because downtrodden souls reek of slothfulness and Smirnoff. A man is less than a man and more mud when he allows his body to become one with the earth. But nature has a way of weeding out bad seeds that think they can bloom and shine for free. Getting a job is easy, so why not clean yourself up and make the simple choice to exchange destitution for restitution? No matter, this park is the perfect place to sit for families to enjoy a picnic lunch after Sunday service and mingle with members of society—because loving thy neighbor as thyself is the second-most important commandment behind loving thy God.

Proof of Life

Do you know what I want? I want justice - oceans of it. I want fairness - rivers of it. That's what I want. That's all I want.

– Amos 5:24

I don't want to talk about my fickle prostrate,
or the lowball offers for my bike listed on eBay,
or about a white cop that was finally found guilty of
     murder.
So instead, let's discuss the tip of an iceberg,
and how 90% of its body is rooted underwater,
submerged and suppressed like generations of voices
while the other 10% is kinda like a raised fist saying
        I'm still here.
But I don't' want to talk about math.
So instead let's talk about
the chasm between facts and opinions
and the different ways to define
the space between
     figurative   and   literal
    tighten and twist
   noose and neck.

There are days I get so angry I just wanna
scream and scrub the stain from my skin
because the residue from my divorce
can still be found dripping off my fingertips
and bleeding into my days and on a similar note,
I've always maintained the saddest day of the week
is always the day after

because that's when you've had time to think
and evaluate which pieces are too plentiful
to ever be
picked back up.

We do the best with what we can and call it
learning.
We hug our own bodies tight and call it
damage control.

The sun rises again and shines on our faces
and we are fortunate enough to be greeted
with another opportunity to mess up again,
or another chance to speak life
into what we thought we'd already
murdered,
and we all shine and melt into
        tomorrow.

Desiring Sunlight

I knew I was too old to go down the hill even before I
slammed on the brakes and flipped over the handlebars
as the asphalt awaited to high-five
           my sliding body.

I understood how vernacular of the day changes,
but the meaning is never outdated as I whispered, *YOLO*,
deciding pride outweighed preservation and I descended
as if the failure to do so would be worse than
the fall.

Because the body has the capacity to put itself
back together; pain is never to drawn to scale,
but just how is the ego
          reassembled?
How many badges do our puffed-out chests wear
that we didn't truly
earn?

The physician examined me during my follow-up
and advised, *Use pain as your guide.*
And I wish someone with a doctorate in Life would've
been that direct long ago
so I could've saved myself from going up and down
hills and valleys that resulted in scars
that still itch
today.

I inspect the plant in the living room that keeps
losing its leaves despite my providing a
generous supply of water and wonder how much air

a man needs to breathe,
how long it takes for that same man
to wilt.

In a Time of Restlessness

My wife says she doesn't dream, and my spirit animal is the world's biggest concern. I've never had the misfortune of simply living as being a cross to bear, but I sympathize with the bodies of black men being fed to bullets. Closing your eyes to the plight of a breath is equivalent to biting your tongue, though your teeth have fallen out long ago. Not even the most spiteful virus can quarantine the hate created from the vines of a bad seed. Regularly talking to plants not only helps them grow but controls the temper(ament) of your own voice. Soft pastels are the most prominent shades seen when one is sleeping, but she doesn't even see those. How can a man give up when it's clear he's already surrendered? Even nightmares know when enough is enough.

Meditation

What intrigues me most on my stroll around the park
is the group of geriatrics doing tai chi,
brittle limbs dancing in tune to a slow-motion
symphony.

I admire their activity in a world of comfort which I imagine
helps them balance out the yin and yang of their golden years
filled with moments of tarnishment
and a longevity of luster.

But I wonder what happens when they die.
Are they replaced by a younger, sprier senior,
or does that spot remain empty in tribute to a body
that stayed in motion up until the moment
life left?

I've reached an age where my spine is no longer
always aligned with the actions of my body,
and my 40s is a race between preventing and treating
lower back pain, and a weekly trip to the chiropractor
is as satisfying as the well-done red meat I ate last night,
as well as several nights before, which I know
my doctor will politely point out at
my next checkup.

But what's a life without treating yourself for the
victories that may not have ever even seemed like
potential battles, yet now present themselves each day,
such as nagging indigestion
or a stubborn lumbar?

How many meals of baked potatoes and steak has the
woman in the wheelchair waving her arms
like they're taming the wind
eaten while not regretting
the contents of her menu?

I hope I'm able to stand in a circle of my peers and
practice an ancient martial art during my final days
as a way to tell my body,
*Thanks for the protection, but it's now okay
to let go of my soul.*

Visibility

There is no negotiation between the calm and the storm. No handshake is consummated before the two fuse together, digress, and diverge from tranquility to tempest. I've seen many a man go his separate way, but his measure is determined by the realization that he finally needs to stop and ask for directions. *Excuse me, where can I wobble though the straight and wedge amongst the narrow?* The forecast can call for rain, but what matters most is if the puddle is seen as a means of diversion or drowning. Splish-splash I was taking a bath, or whiplash—I can't help but continue to look back. In those instances, the trick is to make friends with your ghosts. Invite them over for a round of cornhole and some zesty guac. Play air guitar during their attempts at karaoke. Be the host other hauntings talk about. Unfortunately, even the most water repellant umbrella can't keep you totally dry from the sudden downpour of a pity party. In those instances, ration your hope and get to higher ground. There is no bargaining between an act and God.

Cleansing

My physical revealed my body is working
as it should,
everything properly connecting and circulating
through me as if induction into middle-age
is a commitment I'm honoring
with each reluctant trip to the Y and
consistent bedtime,
though my attention span shortens each year
and I lack the patience to scroll through
my social media feed
reading the details of yet another
        mass shooting.

My pastor says we must continue to
pray for our country.
But how can anyone keep their eyes closed at a time
                                    such as this?

Last night I dreamt I was
chewing on glass,
spitting out shards like events from my past
that left a bad taste in my mouth,
blood dripping down my chin
like taking shots of bitterness which are
no longer compatible with my taste buds and
temperament.

This morning I stared through the bathroom mirror,
tracing lines extending outward from
the corners of my eyes that can be classified
as roads of recklessness
or recovery and I know

we are not the same men we once were concerning
the fire
before
the baptism.

The Yips

The second baseman can no longer make
a simple throw to first
        without bouncing the ball in the dirt
or chucking it in either direction down the line,
as if he can't remember the mechanics of the relationship
between father and son and their front yard
                        in the summers.

The manager tells his guy to just play and relax whenever
his nerves hijack his talent
because overthinking has killed many a mood,
and a career.

Some claim it's psychological,
that the brain ignores the trajectory of muscle memory
and no matter how many extra pre-game grounders
the player takes, the result will be the same,
because despite our best intentions,
the mistakes we make in our lives are simply recorded as
        errors in any box score.

Sometimes when the ball is hit to me,
a sharp liner out to left field,
I freeze when I know my wife is upset
because I'm unsure what to say,
and my efforts at consolation end in a soft lob
that doesn't nearly reach her
or a wayward rocket that nails her in the gut,
too hot for her to possibly handle.

We become scared to attempt the simple throws
when we forget the fundamentals,
when our minds and bodies convince each other
they aren't on the same team and
the connection between the two is as distant as
hapless player and die-hard fan
screaming at the TV after yet
another letdown.

The second baseman,
the newlywed husband,
the grizzled manager who knows from experience,
sometimes you just gotta ride it out,
let the ball go where it may
understanding there's always another season for redemption
        just waiting on the next play.

Physics

There's poetry, there's Presbyterians, and look, there's a piano soaring overhead in the vastness of sky! It floats like a baseball swatted by a cleanup hitter, yet this object isn't made of cowhide but of mahogany and the relic of a grandmother's den. One minute you're looking up as if examining clues leading to religion or rain, the next minute you see a baby grand silhouetted amidst the horizon. Sometimes it's not important to ascertain the *hows* or *whys*, but to enjoy the elevation of *what ifs*. Unlike a plane getting lost in the clouds, the instrument's path is clearly visible, as if skywriting a song with a chorus that goes something like, "Hear me when I say, you can believe in what seems too lovely, to be truuuuue," before crashing to the earth to the tune of wood and keys colliding in perfect harmony for the occasion, a celebration denoting loss and being found. It's appropriate to say a prayer equal to the weight of the situation. Now bow your heads. The bigger they are, the harder they follow the laws of gravity and God.

Father's Day

for Devan and Maya

I'm still learning how to navigate the terrain between
fatherhood and second wife,
as if my new moral compass can direct my steps
amongst cracks and chasms,
despite perception being often greater than
    the divide.

The man in the Starbucks parking lot yells
to another man hoisting his dog from his car
how beautiful of a black Lab she is
and the hoister yells back,
Not a white hair in her!
She was actually born on Halloween.
Best dog I've ever had!
And I think of people who call October 31st
their favorite holiday,
    wondering if that day even IS a holiday,
and maybe because every day I miss my kids,
but I realize my favorite day of the year is now
    none.

    How a man measures up to his own life
    can be calculated once he finally reveals his
        degrees of grief.

    How he handles moving forward depends on
    when he's finally able to milk the memories from
        the mourning.

My stepdaughter's dog continues to walk around
in circles and my wife says that's what they do when
they're looking for a place
to die.
But there are times in our lives when we all
walk around in circles,
looking for our own place to fall
and then get back up...
                    or not.

My kids joined my wife and I for dinner
this year for Father's Day,
and no amount of costumes, or turkey,
or shiny presents can coax me into
looking forward to a particular day of the year
any more than the other.

   My ideal day is simply breaking bread with
   my own blood, laughing with those who
   share my last name,
   and biting into a well-done piece of meat,
   as if all the flavors came together
   especially for that meal.

The Farmer's Market of Fresh Decadence

Bearded men in Birkenstocks flock to select the choicest of rutabaga because it's Saturday morning and the husbands and wives regard today as the sabbath of agriculture as they stroll about and admire the deliberateness of the jicama, the tenacity of the radishes. There must be some sort of symbiotic relationship in the ogling of produce picked by migrant hands, but what of the middleman who is caught between a world of well-to-do consumer and meager producer? Is it still exploitation when a paycheck determines each party has no choice but to RSVP? But the husbands and wives only know there will be fresh veggies on the table and the route of the food plays no part in the preparation of dinner when they bow their heads and thank the Lord for this meal.

Transparency

The homeless filter in and out of Starbucks—a motley
crew of discarded Grandes and Ventis who order free ice

water, charge their old phones, and spend an excessive
amount of time cleaning up in bathrooms the baristas

frown upon entering because they're forced to mop
what's left of a mess from the newest residents. I sit in

an uncomfortable wooden chair in the corner and watch
a Netflix show in which a man confined to a wheelchair,

for the first time, faces the man who shot him, paralyzing
him from the waist down. And I recall when I sat across

from my ex-wife in the coffeeshop and apologized for
every shot I ever fired at her during our marriage, leaving

her paralyzed, herself, because I'm sorry was a bullet she'd
never been struck with. Sometimes humility and forgiveness

are the same shade of grace, different hues of blue that
mold into the same background of clouds that weren't

there to hide your view of a world you thought you had
to have, but existed to protect you from the effects of

its harmful rays. Today I think about how I always tell
my wife not to text while she's driving and she tells me

she's learning how to navigate my stubbornness, and
together we travel down our beautiful open road of

iPhones and irony. The Uber Eats driver picks up an

order of lattes and coffee cake and will deliver them
to someone who has chosen convenience over extra

fees, and it's amazing how advanced technology has
made us, the way our food can be passed directly from

provider to driver to consumer which goes to show
just how hungry we are.

Hangman

Is there a

B

as in buoyancy, as in floating to the top when the design is to anchor certain people down (which happens to rhyme with drown). As in breath, like, I can't breathe because a knee to the neck is not conducive to the plight of any airway. Not as in *bee* like the freedom to stop and smell the roses and then fly away to any neighborhood of your choosing. But *Be* as in *Be careful. Be compliant. Beware.*

How about an

L

as in loss, as in mourning, as in another son gone by way of gun. As in lost, as in the police officer got lost in prejudiced thought and mistook a taser with a Glock on the body of the young man whose death sparked yet another protest. As in taking one for the team, as in the translation of *one* is a bullet and translation of *the team* is another name added to a history of hashtags.

Give me an

A

as in again, as in how many more. As in aftermath, as in the crime scene cordoned off by yellow tape like an inner-city halo because all the angels in town cry out for justice. As in the power of prayer must include action and activism, otherwise it's simply a plea and *Please stop killing* is not even close to being a loose paraphrasing of the commandment because it clearly states *Thou shall not kill.*

I'll take a

C

as in color, as in stay in the lines, as in showing your true shades of hate. As in calling the kettle what you can't be so you won't ever understand how it feels to finally reach your boiling point. As in crime, as in misdemeanor is never grounds for murder, as in conspiracy, as in collusion, as in telling your partners to turn off their body cameras. As in bypassing judge and jury due to fitting the proverbial description, skipping straight to executioner.

I know there's a

K

as in this is not oKay.
   This is not oKay.
  This is not... oKay.

Year in Review

Just after Christmas the newscaster lamented,
This has been a year to forget, as if memories can be
sifted and strained with a colander for the brain.

But I'm inclined to believe that purposely failing
to remember is like throwing the entire contents
of your soul down the garbage disposal when all

you really had to do was wait and see what you
could prepare from the leftovers. In my dream
last night, my son and daughter floated with me

in an ocean, and when my daughter said, *I wonder
how deep it is,* I wanted to reply, *Pretty darn deep,*
however, I didn't want my experience with

darkness and depths to taint their views of
buoyancy. A father can teach his children how
to swim, but what's more important is guiding

them in how not to drown. The college running
back who died in an accidental shooting over the
weekend obviously didn't mean to put a bullet in

his abdomen, yet I imagine his mother wishes she
would've warned him just once more of the effects
of gun control. And at the beginning of each year,

resolutions are made that will never be kept, because what good is a promise to yourself when you can't recall the certainty of hurt, the shade of failure.

Binge-Watching
For Tyre

While viewing the reality show in which contestants
make knives from piles of metal, I think of the latest

group of police officers posing as contestants on their
own reality show where they compete by beating and

hammering out their victims, not to create an edge
sharp enough to slice through water bottles and sugar

cane, but to see which cop can deliver a kill shot of
their own. At the end of round one, the blades are

presented to the judges and whoever created the blade
that needs the most correction is eliminated, while in

round one, the cop on the scene that shows the most
acts of compassion is gone. In round two, handles are

added for grasping and the creator of the knife that
hurts the hand while being wielded is sent home and

in round two, the man in blue who tries to grip his
colleague into submission after repeated body blows

to the victim is asked not to return to the division.
The final round consists of the forgers returning

home to replicate a sword or ax or other weapon used
in battle by an extinct civilization. Upon returning to

the stage and after being tested and evaluated to see who made the most accurate and devastatingly brutal

replica, the winner is selected and awarded $10,000, while the winning police officer is determined by who

gets the most media coverage and who abused their authority in the worst way all while finding the most innocent man to murder.

The Main Event

The man standing behind me in Target tells his buddy
his workplace is creating a fight club,
and I wonder if hands will be thrown in the name of
middle management and manhood
or if the employees will simply be arguing back and forth,
pointing fingers like political parties stressing
just how wrong
      the other one is.

I recently read about a man dying immediately after
entering a taco-eating contest.
The coroner officially listed choking as the cause of death,
but what are the odds the autopsy would also show
ego and competition are
kindred spirits?

        I understand the dynamics of blowing off steam.
        I've studied how the mouth forms a shape just small
        enough to free the air from the toxic body,
        but large enough to proclaim and pronounce
                                glory.

I struggle with how much of my personal life
to share in a poem.
Should I say how the fissures from my own darkness
spread until I was ready to stop lamenting
the curvature of imperfect lines,

finally ready to plug the cracks
and resurrect the foundation?
Or should I just say,
   Earthquakes suck, man.

Is there a Richter scale that ranges from self-pity to rehabilitation?
How well can you withstand
what is eating you alive?
It's often a case of self vs. selfless,
the poet vs. the person,
picking your punches
as if the next uppercut to the gut
      could end it all.

Hunting

Gone are the days of being voted *Most likely to catch a tiger by the toe*. Always the wild cat tamer attempting to snare an appendage... never the prom queen. Though there's something to be said for being recognized amongst the habitat of your peers as a go-getter of exotic animals. But a bridesmaid begins to develop a complex when she's only as good as the groomsman she's paired up with. When you're an accessory to the photo, you smile through the pain because those are not the shoes you would've chosen. A soul is composed of being and belief, but a blister is the result of friction grating against thin skin. Putting on a pretty face is akin to dressing for both sorrow and success. If I had a word to leave behind in my election acceptance it would be this, *Catch the undomesticated beast by the toe, no matter how loud he hollers ... never let him go.*

Little League Position Primer

Pitcher (1)

Often the biggest and most talented. Best arm on the team. A steady fastball, a heady game. Wise beyond his age. Perennial All-Star. Nothing to do with the fact that he's almost always the coach's son. Also, one of the strongest hitters and will continue to be so until college. Plays short when not blowing away tweens in the summer. Plays quarterback and walks with his pretty girlfriend over vermillion leaves during the fall.

Catcher (2)

The burliest, sturdiest boy. Squats down for six innings because twelve-year-old tendons never tire. Checks the hitter's eyes to make sure he's not stealing signs and flashes fingers that flicker like flashlight. One: heater. Two: curve: Three: "The (insert pitcher's first name) Special."

First Baseman (3)

The biggest boy, but never pitches because his balls skid in the dirt more than they split the strike zone. Able to stretch and snag throws over his head with gangly arms that dangle at his side like awkward apologies, throws headed towards Toledo. Often the clean-up hitter. RBI machine who the opposing parents claim, "Has gotta be at least fifteen."

Second Baseman (4)

Scrappy kid with a heart bigger than Wrigley Field. Golden glove that gobbles up grounders. The first one to cry when the team loses. The last one to change out of his dusty uniform after the game. Stat freak who could recite the longest hitting streak of every current starter for every major league team. Wears team cap to school and puts his favorite ballplayer's baseball card under the bill. A weak hitter, almost last in the lineup, but a slap-bunt specialist. The smallest body, but the biggest mouth. Dreams of the Big Leagues harder than anyone else. Counts box scores instead of sheep. Turns double-plays in his sleep. *4-6-3... 4-6-3.*

Third Baseman (5)

Strapping youth built for stopping one-hoppers with his chest. Cocky keeper of the hot corner. Hybrid doubles and home-run hitter. Potential to play any position. Shotgun arm gunning down runners before they reach the bag. Most likely to succeed at the next level.

Shortstop (6)

See Pitcher.

Left Field (7)

Not necessarily a spot designated for the clueless kid. Slow runner. Not good with grounders. Often fat. But able to handle a bat. Resident funny guy who drives in his share of laughs and RBI.

Center Field (8)

Ideal lead-off hitter. Often the most inner-city kids since they're usually the fastest. Speedy child who swipes bases and never looks back. This will serve him well should he decide to sacrifice baseball for other sports. Sports where his lucrative legs slow down just enough to position him for first-round draft status.

Right Field (9)

It's no coincidence it's designated the last spot in the field; also last in batting. Where the worst ballplayers go to hide, and eventually die. Position designated for the subs who (by rule) must play at least two innings in the field. Sometimes these kids want to sign up. Most often it's their dads who want them to play. A ball hit to them is at least a double. Odds are, equal number of balls will be overran or fumbled. The crowd goes crazy at the routine play. Teammates understand who is out there and find it futile to complain. Never the coach's son.

Windmill

She winds up and launches herself forward
the way her private coach has taught her to,
as if the blur of her swinging limbs
is sure to deliver a strike to the center
of his squatting body.
But the balls bounce before they reach his glove,
as if each pitch suffers a mid-air coronary,
each bounce a gasping last breath.
The lessons are not working.
Forty dollars, thirty minutes a week,
and she can barely reach the
thirty-five-foot distance from the mound
to home.

His first reaction is to chastise her
for not being able
to hurl the ball across the plate
the way the others coach's daughters do,
to chide her for not generating the velocity
he did when he was a kid,
a fourth grade phenom who bloomed,
wilted, then gained new life through
        his son.

    He played two years before quitting,
    before he could no longer tolerate being told
    that he could do better,
    before being lectured that his carefree
    childhood efforts were a reflection
    of his father.

He's an older and wiser target for her
than he was for him, a matured dad
who understands that his lower back will ache
tomorrow,
who knows that his knees are more bum than
ever before.

He has learned to ignore
each ball skidding in the dirt,
learned to save his lectures for more pressing
issues that will, no doubt, occur much later
during her teenage years
because he knows each pitch is
simultaneously,
his girl's best attempt and
a daughter's apology.

Faster and Noticeably More Furious

I admit it's been a while since I watched a film
in the franchise, so I know I've missed a lot in

between sagas: births and deaths and resurrections,
street racing evolving to makeshift space missions.

I understand, firsthand, our lives all have sequels
in which plot twists occur, even though in a sense

we write our own scripts. But in which movie
did gearheads turn murderers? When did guns

become an addition to stick shifts? Somewhere in
the series, what began as friends sipping Coronas in

an Echo Park backyard segued into semi-automatics
used for self-defense in a Central American jungle.

Somewhere in my own story, I stopped to consider
the necessity of shots fired and the placement of

bullets and realized the only true target audience
is yourself. So how does the Toretto bloodline,

a map of open byways and highways, not speak to
every nerve in Dom's body pleading with him that

the finish line is only as sweet as the muscle car that
brought you there, and that the message isn't really

to go big, but to simply go home. We are taught to
keep our foot on the pedal and not let up, but in that

way are unable to savor the gust of air from the
checkered flag. Instead, we slide our hands across

our foreheads to wipe the sweat from cleaving a
machete through the fronds of our own Amazon

as if violence is our only way out.

Blackout

How lovely the sky is after a few days
of rioting

hues of bleeding coral simultaneously merging
and bursting with fury and hurt

in protest of what we deserve
but may never have

as if it knows this won't be the last time
a black man dies from blue hands

and so we look up to savor every last second
as if looting the sunset
                              for all its worth.

Down Here on the Ground

after Wes Montgomery

Cue the static that rubs like nerves against the desired grain. Note how the vinyl crackles like feeding notes to the fire, though each authentic sacrifice can be told solely from the gravity of its own ashes. Every sound is wrapped in a plea and prayer, regardless of the plight. The 11th commandment in essence states *That which isn't audible must be regarded as pliable to the touch.* If rhythm were to replicate itself, it would be to the tune of improvisational hopscotch on loop. So many anxious toes, so little time for tapping. There is not enough jazz to capture the rhapsody of summer, to frame the fragrance of wilting lilies, to fade out like a grieving sunset in search of the next mourning.

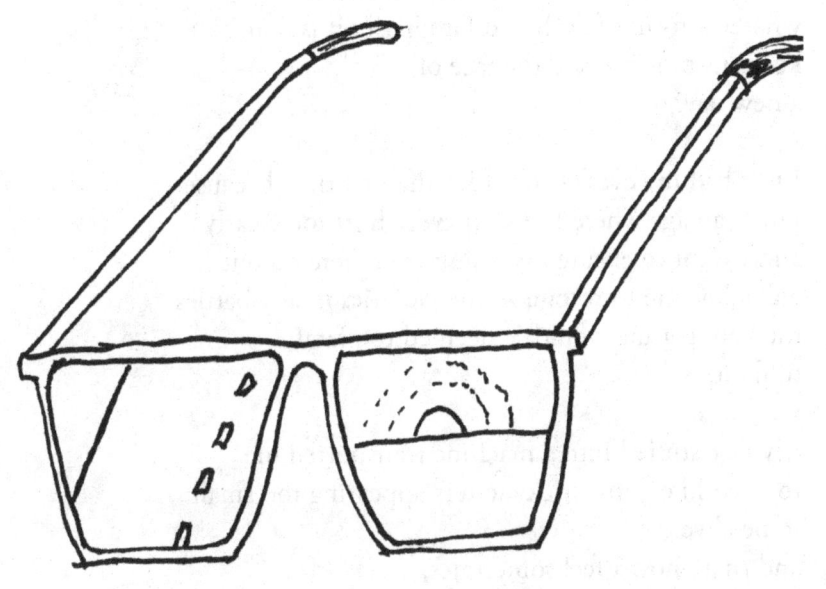

20/20

When the regular asked how she was doing
the barista replied, *Living the dream,* before making
his usual drink,
and isn't that what we all do as we rely on
whatever form of faith and familiarity it is that
keeps us moving into the face of
a new day?

I just had my eyes checked for the first time because
I'm at an age where I've seen every hurt too clearly
and I want to ensure my vision from here on out
will allow me to recognize the victories in any battles
the younger me would've deemed too fatal
to fight.

My face stuffed into a machine transported me
to a world of tiny, tricky letters appearing too small
to be alive
and that's how I feel sometimes,
overcome by a combination of consonants and vowels
teaming together to create sounds that still echo
amongst memories clanking around in a life
I've left behind but will never
forget.

Shouldn't we all aspire to attain the stillness of the barista,
the one who makes the same drinks and repeats the process
in the midst of monotony,
her fears and misgivings swirling around inside each cup
like a never-ending threatening motion

before eventually settling at the bottom
rather than us guessing at a series of blurry symbols in our lives
trying to guess at
what we can't see?

Her customer leaves and thanks her for his purchase and for
her sense of reverie and the barista says,
I'll keep it as long as I can,
and the optometrist says I'll need reading glasses
in the next few years,
both of us making out all that is in front of us
the way we want to see it
whether in the distance,
or right under
our noses.

Leisure

This old man came rolling home, but *that* old man remains impeccably dressed sitting on a park bench eating an egg salad sandwich. Who could blame the guy for not wanting to risk breaking a hip and soiling his new fedora? This old man had things to do, TV shows to watch, a bedtime awaiting. It's not like *that* old man didn't also have a routine to adhere to. But being by yourself is cause for getting lost in regimen or in clouds where children's feet dip in and out of Heaven. I believe in just desserts and judgment day, but I'll never condemn a man for the way he chooses to live out his isolation. To each his lone. Mothers rushed to gather their toddlers from his path, and this old man rolled down sweeping hills and across busy boulevards just in time to water his begonias. But *that* old man is in no rush. He knows tomorrow it will rain. Lunch will be ham on rye. And before he leaves for the day, knick knack paddy whack or not, he will give the dog a bone.

Yelp

I walked the perimeter of the furniture store
looking for a couch I already knew I wouldn't buy
due to the bad reviews I read online,
but I was already in the parking lot
and too often convenience
outweighs conscience.

The saleswoman told me,
That was fast, right before I exited,
and if I'd have been introspective enough
I would've responded,

> *That's what happens when you realize you deserve*
> *greater than upholstery that will cave in on you when*
> *you need a soft spot to rest more so than ever.*

If only it were that easy to move in, around,
and back out of the lives of the ones we thought
were there for the betterment of our buoyancy,
but who actually allowed us to sink even deeper
into ourselves.

The plot of the movie I just saw about time travel
was too confusing to follow,
however maybe that's the point,
not being able to retrace steps so you can forget
the way back to where it was
you were never meant to repair.

It's as if the algorithms lined up to do—

something or other, and you were spared
to have been told nothing by your future self
that could alter the course of a purchase
you had to make
just so your words
could warn others.

Braille
for Juanita

My wife and in-laws say their goodbyes to their
        grandmother
while she lies still and listens to words
that funnel into closure
because family trees are covered in sap
that sticks and stains
and I recall the times in my life
I thought were un-survivable and think,
        Can one sleep in a deathbed while they are living?

Last night we sat on the couch and watched a movie
where a father narrated pieces of his childhood
to his daughter and I wonder what my own kids
will tell their children about the memories
they made with me while
                    I still lived in their house.

Each night before bed, I look at pictures of vintage bikes
I want to buy because it's my way of mourning
the passing of my childhood,
    as if buying something so old, so used,
    and then restoring it lessens the effect of
    rust coating the body that's too stuck to ever
    remove.

When someone leaves the world, we claim
they're looking down on us, but in that way
                  we are liars

because possessing an angelic soul is the utmost in
empathy and there is no such thing as
hurting in Heaven.

So we say our farewells to loved ones,
          adios to the good old days,
                    and trace spots glued to our skin
no amount of scrubbing
will ever get out.

Dromedary

Listen. It's not that the camel is incapable of being anything more than what it is. We know only so much straw can be placed upon the sturdiest backs before they give way to the weight. It's more so that this grand ship of the desert plodding through the dunes guided by mirages and moonlight is actually the romanticized version of a mother from Sheboygan lugging three kids through the Costco checkout before hurrying home to prepare a chicken casserole. It's true, camels can go two weeks without water. But the celebrated humps are really mounds of fat used as nourishment so death won't occur when there's no food to be found. Every man thirsts and wanders his own Sahara navigating this lonely stretch of his lifetime. Sometimes he can draw upon reserves to supply himself some form of sustenance amongst the sweltering and starvation. And sometimes his own body cannibalizes itself in an effort to conceal the burn from the skin. To draw a line in the sand is to say enough is enough. To bury your head in it is to lay the groundwork for your own ashes.

Conceding

The day after the election votes are still being
counted,
and the man walking ten feet to my right whose shoes
look like they've seen better decades
has a conversation with himself and with those
who appear to be all the men
he used to be.

Pundits are counting the sum of red and blue states
trying to cast a light the color of layman's terms
so we can be at ease with at least
accepting the fate
of our next four years.

The mumbling man says, *Gotta' do better*,
and for a moment I wonder if he's speaking of himself
or the nation, and when he yells, *To hell with it!*
I know our country
is in danger.

There is talk the president won't vacate his position if
defeated,
and sometimes force is the only way we learn
the control we think we have is a fleeting term
modeled by the manner in which we acquire
loss.

I'm drawn back to the man to my right,
the independent thinker with the size 11 soiled shoes
because our souls, too, bear the filth

of so much tread and mudslinging,
and I wonder if either candidate
will be able to help
any of us at all.

Full Count

Her pitches loop over home plate
like exhausted planets
fatigued from the weight of gravity.

I pace the dugout back and forth,
more concerned father
than assistant coach.
Worrying more for her performance
than our team box score.

With each pitch I become the ball:
starry-eyed sphere waiting to be belted
into the outfield,
where teammates give chase:
the beginning of lives relying
on the hands of others to get them out of jams,
hands designed to commit errors
through no fault of their own.

Every time a batter misses,
overzealous swings slicing air—
a reprieve,
each strike equaling living another day.
And every time she strikes out another man's daughter,
I smile.

Now I understand why some fathers are never to be found
during the last inning of games,
reappearing just in time to watch the coach
hand out game balls.

Every baseball idiom was created
when a man's child was on the mound.

    Behind in the count.
    One base at a time.
    It ain't over till it's over.

My babygirl struggles to throw strikes.
The umpire must not have kids.
Everything in life
is hit,
or miss.

Stickball

Summers were a never-ending 7th inning,
and games stretched into the next day
when the sun no longer lit the cul-de-sac.

My brother's knuckleball was an
experiment in flight pattern,
a taunting array of speculation:

            juking and jutting,
      a hovering slow dance
                        inventing new steps
the batter could never learn.

My fastball was a humming blur of rocket science.

And whomever made contact deserved to
commandeer the moon.

The neighborhood kids were filler,
Portuguese soccer-playing
perpetual strikeout victims
always stuck in right field
because they were more skilled
with their feet than
with their hands.

Today it's the bottom of the 9th inning.
Two outs.

And we are dreamers posing as fathers

reminding our own children,
"Point your toe to the target.

Keep your elbow up.
And follow through on the pitch."

Today I remember belting an old tennis ball
over the neighbor's roof
into his backyard,

gliding around makeshift bases
with glorious fists raised
as if God was pulling our hands.

Fumes

For Edward

I spent Saturday exhaling embers from a Friday night
sitting around Ed's fire pit. When men get together,

they cough up truths only revealed through smoke and
mirrors that reflect themselves, and the burning of wood

and grilling of steaks creates a camaraderie that doubles
as good eats and therapy. I like my meat very well done

and since the Bible states that's what the Lord will tell
you if you make it to Heaven, I can accept being shamed

for desiring a more charred sustenance. Flavor and faith
are subjective, but one should never allow another man's

tastes to dictate his pallet. We grub and philosophize into
the night under stars that struggle to be celebrated and seen

because a surplus of streetlights creates an artificial beauty,
but a cold drink and breaking bread with a brother in these

conditions is still a religious experience, a backyard kind of
communion. Ed talks of making his pit smokeless and I

express wanting a new teaching job, and the ash in our hair
and glowing grey in our beards is our résumé showing all

that we've learned.

9th Inning

The singer and the actor have reunited after a two-decade
hiatus in which rappers and athletes and divorces have

interrupted the moments in between their first kiss and
most recent sighting on the red carpet as if their newest

merger is an advertisement for indecisiveness and mid-life
crisis and makes me wonder if there's an expiration date

on loneliness, because to jump from person to person is
not a lost art, but an art in loss. And when the barista told

me she'd never be part of a marriage again because of all
the paperwork that accompanies the end of one, I pondered

if her half-empty coffee cup outlook would always be
worth the cost of never even considering a refill. My

favorite baseball team's closer continues to blow saves
and his manger continues to send him out at the end

of games which in non-baseball vernacular translates to
Your boyfriend still hasn't proposed, and you want to believe the

next month is when he'll finally take your hints to heart. But what
we are willing to accept for ourselves and what we want is

the equivalent of dropping to a knee locked in limbo,
either having the strength to return to a standing position

or allowing our body to just fall face-first into the earth. Sometimes we need to be the one to walk out of the

dugout towards the pitcher's mound, take the ball away and say, "Kenley. Thanks... but you're done."

ACKNOWLEDGMENTS

433: The Park of Pretentiousness

As it Ought to be Magazine: 20/20, The Main Event

Autofocus: Father's Day

Cutleaf: 9th Inning, Faster and Noticeably More Furious

Decomp: Stickball

Elevation Review: Proof of Life

Gone Lawn: Physics, Visibility

HAD: Little League Primer, Sign Stealing, Windmill

Indolent Books: Conceding

LittleDeath Lit: Cleansing

Mobius: Blackout

MORIA: Variations

Nassau Review: Leisure

New Verse News: Pigeon-Watching

Oddball Magazine: Zenith

Pigeonholes: Fumes

Pine Hills Review: Year in Review

Rigorous: Braille

Sledgehammer: Desiring Sunlight

Somos en Escrito: Down Here on the Ground

Sparks of Calliope: Transparency

Split Rock Review: Dromedary

Subnivean: Meditation, What You Wouldn't Believe but Should, Yelp, The Yips

Rise Up Review: Hangman

Thimble Literary Magazine: Hi Five

Topical Poetry: Front Page

Trestle Ties: In a Time of Restlessness

Ucity Review: Hunting

Your Daily Poem: Full Count

AUTHOR BIO

Daniel Romo is the author *Moonlighting as an Avalanche* (Tebot Bach 2021), *Apologies in Reverse* (FutureCycle Press 2019), *When Kerosene's Involved* (Mojave River Press 2014), and *Romancing Gravity* (Silver Birch Press 2013). His writing and photography can be found in The Los Angeles Review, Yemassee, Hotel Amerika, Barrelhouse, and elsewhere. He received an MFA from Queens University of Charlotte, and he lives and teaches in Long Beach, CA. More at danieljromo.com.